CONFLICTED BUT LOYAL

Conflicted but Loyal

Walter the Educator

Silent King Books

Silent King Books

SKB

Copyright © 2024 by Walter the Educator

All rights reserved. No part of this book may be reproduced in any manner whatsoever without written permission except in the case of brief quotations embodied in critical articles and reviews.

First Printing, 2024

Disclaimer
This book is a literary work; poems are not about specific persons, locations, situations, and/or circumstances unless mentioned in a historical context. This book is for entertainment and informational purposes only. The author and publisher offer this information without warranties expressed or implied. No matter the grounds, neither the author nor the publisher will be accountable for any losses, injuries, or other damages caused by the reader's use of this book. The use of this book acknowledges an understanding and acceptance of this disclaimer.

This little collectible short story is dedicated to those that are loyal...

Mr. Jonathan Fields was the epitome of dedication. A teacher at Crestwood High School for over a decade, he was beloved by students and respected by colleagues. Every morning, Jonathan arrived at dawn, coffee in hand, ready to inspire young minds. His passion for history was infectious, turning even the most reluctant students into avid learners.

Conflicted but Loyal

At home, Jonathan's life seemed lifted from a fairy tale. His wife, Claire, was the picture of perfection: supportive, kind, and endlessly patient. They met in college and married soon after graduation. Their relationship was one of seamless harmony, filled with laughter, shared dreams, and unwavering support. They had two children, Emily and Jack, who were the apple of Jonathan's eye.

Conflicted but Loyal

However, life has a way of stirring up old memories, even in the most content hearts. It was a crisp autumn morning when the winds of change blew through Crestwood High. Jonathan was adjusting his tie in the staff room mirror when he heard a familiar voice.

Conflicted but Loyal

"Jonathan? Is that really you?"

Conflicted but Loyal

He turned, and his breath caught in his throat. Standing there, with the same spark in her eyes and an aura that seemed to make the room glow, was Rachel Monroe. Rachel had been Jonathan's first love, a whirlwind romance that ended abruptly when she moved away. They lost touch, as often happens with youthful passions, but the imprint she left on his heart remained.

Conflicted but Loyal

"Rachel," he stammered, trying to keep his composure. "I had no idea you'd be here."

Conflicted but Loyal

"I just got the job," she replied, her smile as radiant as ever. "I'll be teaching English. It's great to see you again."

Conflicted but Loyal

Over the next few weeks, Jonathan found it increasingly difficult to concentrate. Memories of late-night talks, shared dreams, and youthful indiscretions flooded back. Every time he saw Rachel in the hallway, a pang of nostalgia tugged at him. Claire noticed a change in him, though she never pried. She trusted him implicitly, which only made Jonathan feel guiltier for his wandering thoughts.

Conflicted but Loyal

One evening, after putting Emily and Jack to bed, Jonathan sat on the porch, lost in thought. Claire joined him, her presence a soothing balm.

Conflicted but Loyal

"Jonathan, is everything alright?" she asked gently, her hand resting on his.

Conflicted but Loyal

He sighed, the weight of his internal conflict pressing down on him. "Claire, you know I love you more than anything. But Rachel... she's back, and it's stirred up so many old memories. I feel so confused."

Conflicted but Loyal

Claire listened patiently, her eyes filled with understanding. "Jonathan, it's natural to have feelings resurface when someone from your past reappears. But remember, we built this life together. We've shared so much. Don't let nostalgia for what was cloud your vision of what is."

Conflicted but Loyal

Jonathan gazed at her, gratitude swelling in his chest. Claire's words were a reminder of the depth of their bond. He realized that what he had with Claire was not just a fairytale but a partnership built on love, trust, and mutual respect.

Conflicted but Loyal

The next day, Jonathan saw Rachel in the staff room again. This time, he felt a sense of closure rather than confusion. He approached her with a smile, genuine and free of the turmoil that had plagued him.

Conflicted but Loyal

"Rachel, it's wonderful to see you again and to work alongside you. But my heart belongs to my family now. I wish you all the best here at Crestwood."

Conflicted but Loyal

Rachel smiled back, understanding and acceptance in her eyes. "I'm glad you found happiness, Jonathan."

Conflicted but Loyal

With that, Jonathan walked away, feeling lighter than he had in weeks. He returned to his classroom, ready to inspire, knowing that his heart was firmly anchored where it belonged. The past was a cherished memory, but the present was a living, breathing reality, filled with love, commitment, and the joy of a too-good-to-be-true romance that was, in fact, very real.

Conflicted but Loyal

The weeks that followed were a testament to Jonathan's resilience. His renewed focus on teaching and family brought a sense of peace that had been missing. However, life still had a few twists in store for him.

Conflicted but Loyal

One crisp morning, the school buzzed with excitement as preparations for the annual history fair were in full swing. Students scattered about, constructing exhibits and rehearsing presentations. Jonathan, as always, was in the thick of it, guiding his students with patience and enthusiasm.

Conflicted but Loyal

Amid the flurry of activity, Rachel approached him, holding a stack of papers. "Jonathan, could we talk for a moment?"

Conflicted but Loyal

He nodded, a mix of curiosity and apprehension washing over him. They stepped into an empty classroom, the din of the hallway fading behind them.

Conflicted but Loyal

"I wanted to thank you," Rachel began, her voice steady. "Your words the other day helped me more than you know. Moving back here was harder than I expected, and seeing you brought back so many memories. But your honesty gave me the clarity I needed."

Conflicted but Loyal

Jonathan smiled, feeling a sense of closure he hadn't realized he craved. "I'm glad, Rachel. We both needed that conversation."

Conflicted but Loyal

Rachel's eyes brightened with a newfound resolve. "I'm going to be okay, Jonathan. And I think... I think I'll enjoy teaching here."

Conflicted but Loyal

With that, she left, leaving Jonathan with another renewed sense of purpose. He walked back to the bustling hallways, ready to immerse himself in the history fair.

Conflicted but Loyal

That evening, Jonathan returned home to a house filled with the scent of Claire's cooking. The children were playing in the living room, their laughter a comforting melody. As he stepped into the kitchen, he wrapped his arms around Claire from behind, breathing in the familiar scent of lavender and warmth.

Conflicted but Loyal

"Today was a good day," he murmured against her neck.

Conflicted but Loyal

Claire turned, her eyes twinkling. "I'm glad to hear that. How's Rachel doing?"

Conflicted but Loyal

Jonathan chuckled softly. "She's doing well. And so am I, thanks to you."

Conflicted but Loyal

Life at Crestwood High settled into a pleasant rhythm. Jonathan continued to excel in his teaching, and Rachel found her own niche within the school community. Their paths crossed frequently, but the tension had dissolved, replaced by a mutual respect and camaraderie.

Conflicted but Loyal

One day, as spring began to bloom, Crestwood High announced a joint project between the history and English departments. Jonathan and Rachel found themselves collaborating, their shared passion for education creating a seamless partnership. The project flourished, showcasing the best of their combined efforts and bringing new energy to the school.

Conflicted but Loyal

At home, Jonathan and Claire's relationship deepened. They spent evenings discussing their days, planning family outings, and nurturing their children's dreams. Claire's unwavering support and understanding had fortified their bond, making it stronger than ever.

Conflicted but Loyal

One sunny afternoon, as Jonathan watched Emily and Jack play in the yard, Claire joined him on the porch, holding two cups of tea.

Conflicted but Loyal

"Remember when we first moved here?" she asked, handing him a cup.

Conflicted but Loyal

One sunny afternoon, as Jonathan watched Emily and Jack play in the yard, Claire joined him on the porch, holding two cups of tea.

Conflicted but Loyal

"Remember when we first moved here?" she asked, handing him a cup.

Conflicted but Loyal

Jonathan smiled, memories flooding back. "How could I forget? It feels like a lifetime ago."

Conflicted but Loyal

Claire leaned against him, her presence a constant source of comfort. "We've come a long way, haven't we?"

Conflicted but Loyal

He nodded, taking a sip of his tea. "We have. And I wouldn't change a thing."

Conflicted but Loyal

As the sun dipped below the horizon, painting the sky in hues of orange and pink, Jonathan felt a profound sense of gratitude. His journey had been filled with unexpected turns, but it led him to this moment—a life of fulfillment, a career he loved, and a family that meant everything to him.

Conflicted but Loyal

In the end, it wasn't just the memories of his first love that lingered, but the realization that true happiness was found in the here and now, in the love he shared with Claire and the life they built together. And with that knowledge, Jonathan faced each new day with a heart full of contentment and a spirit ready to embrace whatever the future held.

Conflicted but Loyal

About the Creator

Walter the Educator is one of the pseudonyms for Walter Anderson. Formally educated in Chemistry, Business, and Education, he is an educator, an author, a diverse entrepreneur, and he is the son of a disabled war veteran. "Walter the Educator" shares his time between educating and creating. He holds interests and owns several creative projects that entertain, enlighten, enhance, and educate, hoping to inspire and motivate you.

Follow, find new works, and stay up to date with
Walter the Educator™
at WaltertheEducator.com

---

www.ingramcontent.com/pod-product-compliance
Lightning Source LLC
LaVergne TN
LVHW051922060526
838201LV00060B/4124